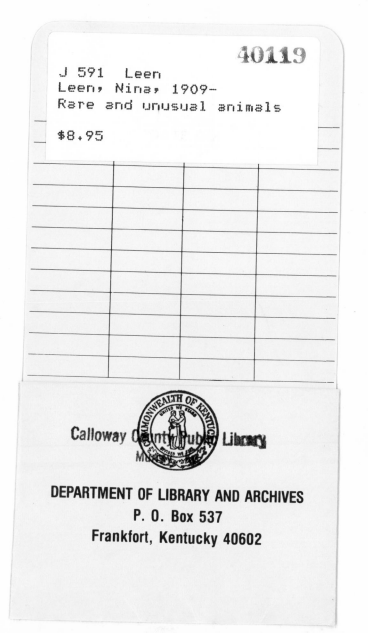

RARE
and UNUSUAL
ANIMALS

by Nina Leen

Holt, Rinehart and Winston / New York

Library of Congress Cataloging in Publication Data
Leen, Nina   Rare and unusual animals.   Includes index.
Summary: Text and photographs introduce a variety
of rare and unusual animals, including tapir, kinkajou,
bongo, Komodo dragon, and many more.
   1. Rare animals—Juvenile literature.
[1. Rare animals]   I. Title   QL83.L45   591
80-22155   ISBN 0-03-057478-1

ACKNOWLEDGMENTS

I am very grateful to
Dr. Karl F. Koopman,
Curator in the Department of Mammalogy
at the American Museum of Natural History
in New York City, for his helpful advice,
welcome criticism, and patience.

I would also like to thank the following people
for their help: Dr. Richard G. Zweifel, Curator
Department of Herpetology
American Museum of Natural History

Members of the New York Zoological Society:
Mr. James G. Doherty,
Curator of Mammals

Mr. Mark MacNamara
Associate Curator of Mammals

Mr. John L. Behler, Curator
Department of Herpetology

Dr. Donald F. Bruning, Curator
Department of Ornithology

I am especially thankful to
Professor Walter W. Dalquest,
Department of Biology,
Midwestern University,
Wichita Falls, Texas,
for introducing me in 1972 to *Coleonyx reticulatus*.
It is probably the only one I will ever meet.

CONTENTS

ANIMALS FEATURED IN THIS BOOK

FOREWORD

A rare animal is usually defined as a species of which only a few are in existence. It is a reasonable definition but it can be misleading.

No one can know how many different animal species exist on earth. Various animals live in remote wilderness areas and it is possible that some species have not yet been discovered. Occasionally, scientific expeditions go into the wild, find a previously unknown species, and bring it back to civilization as a possibly rare animal. But there could be many other such animals in another part of the wild which the expedition did not reach.

Animals that are rarely seen are sometimes assumed to be rare. But species active at night cannot always be detected. They spend the day well camouflaged in woods, hiding in burrows and rocks, or buried in the sand. They move about in the darkness. It is not possible for human beings to see them at night.

It is a sad fact that more and more mammals, birds, and reptiles are becoming rare. Disappearing forests, expanding cities, pollution, killing for profit, and human non-caring threaten the lives of many animals. Some species are common to one region and nonexistent in the rest of the world. Their lives depend on the trees, bushes, grasses, and food sources of the region. If their habitat is threatened by civilized destruction or natural disaster, they cannot move to another place and survive. A once-numerous animal can become rare and eventually perish. Conservationists around the world do all they can to help. They establish wildlife refuges for imperiled animals and fight for laws to protect them.

Once in a while, the reverse happens. A species thought to be extinct years ago suddenly reappears. Where and how it managed to survive is a mystery—with a happy ending.

The giant Panda is the best known rare animal.
It lives in bamboo forests
in remote parts of Western China.

Mammals

NOCTURNAL, ACTIVE AT NIGHT

The *Black-shouldered Opossum* was first discovered in 1950 in the Peruvian rain forest. Only four of these small animals have ever been captured. Nothing definite is known about their way of life.

The *Kinkajou* lives in Central and South America. Its prehensile tail, like a fifth limb, helps it grip branches as it slowly moves from tree to tree in search of food. Mainly a fruit eater, it is especially fond of honey, which explains why it is sometimes called the honey bear.

The *Asiatic Mouse Deer* looks like a toy deer with pencil-thin legs. It has a stomach anatomically similar to that of the camel. The male has long white tusks.

Small and very shy, it is rarely seen by natives.
It moves silently through low undergrowth in the jungle.

The *Pygmy Silky Anteater* lives in the tropics of Central and South America. Climbing above treetops in the rain forest, it feeds on insects, including termites. The long, sticky tongue reaches into the smallest crevices to extract insects.

It rises to defend itself, grasping the branch with its hind feet and prehensile tail. Its front feet have two large, sharp, curved claws. The little anteater is slow and toothless—its claws are its only powerful defense. The eagle-hawk and harpy eagle are its worst enemies.

The *African Palm Civet* sleeps in trees during the day and moves about the forest at night. Its call to other civets sounds like the meow of a kitten.

The civet's short legs with their sharp claws
are well adapted for climbing trees
to look for food. The animals prefer fruits
but will eat rodents, small mammals and birds.

The *Malayan Tapir* lives in tropical forests, near water. It is most active at dusk and dawn. Its chubby, slow-moving appearance is deceiving—it can run, climb, swim and dive. The animal's white coat fools predators: in semidarkness the body's outline is broken up and the head and feet disappear, leaving visible only a shapeless white mass. Fortunately, these gentle plant-eaters are protected by superstition—natives believe that they possess mystical powers.

Baird's Tapir, a native of Central America, is a relative of the Asiatic tapir. Shy and not aggressive, it will defend itself by biting when attacked.

The *Fennec*, the smallest fox, has the largest ears of all foxes. It depends on the sensitivity of its oversized ears to locate live food in the African desert. It eats plants, small rodents, lizards and harmful migratory locusts.

ACTIVE DAY and NIGHT

The *Jaguarondi* is a member of the cat family. Its colors vary from gray to light brown to black. Having neither stripes nor spots it is the only unmarked cat, beside the Puma, in the Americas. Active in trees and on the ground, jaguarondis spend their lives in dense forests.

The *Lesser Panda* inhabits the bamboo forests of Asia. It spends the day sleeping high in trees, occasionally coming down to the ground. Its origin and ancestry are a mystery. Zoologists do not agree on how to classify the animal. Its relation to the giant panda is also under question.

A pair of lesser pandas munch on bamboo sprouts, their favorite food. The lesser panda shares some similarities with raccoons, but a relationship is not certain. Its red fur, white face and long, bushy, ringed tail give it an appealing and unique appearance. The animal is also called the red panda, red cat-bear and Himalayan raccoon.

DIURNAL—ACTIVE DURING THE DAY

The Tree Shrew lives in Asia. Because of certain anatomic characteristics, scientists at first classified it with the primates, the animal order that includes monkeys, apes and man. Later studies made this questionable. It is still undecided as to what order of mammals the animal belongs. The tree shrew's Latin name, *Tupais*, evolved from *toepai*, the Malay word for squirrel. Except for its long snout, it indeed resembles a squirrel.

It takes shelter at night
wherever it finds an opening.

It sits up to eat
or to clean its tail.

From birth the young *Okapi* is a miniature copy of an adult. It inhabits a remote part of the equatorial rain forest of Africa. Shy and well camouflaged under trees by its fur markings, this 500-pound animal was able to remain undetected for centuries.

A female Okapi is seen here with her young.
For years native pygmies told about a mysterious animal that lived deep in the rain forests. They described it as having the back of a zebra, the body of a horse and the neck and head of a giraffe. Zoologists were skeptical of these reports. Around 1900, this "improbable" animal was discovered.

Przewalski's Horses are the only true wild horses surviving today. Very few of them still roam the vast mountainous and desert regions of Mongolia. They are of stocky build, with short legs.

The *Amazon Dolphin* of South America is a mammal that inhabits fresh waters of the Amazon and Orinoco river systems. It differs from its relatives, the marine dolphins, in appearance: it has a long, slightly curved beak with 132–136 teeth, a rounded head, and a flexible neck.

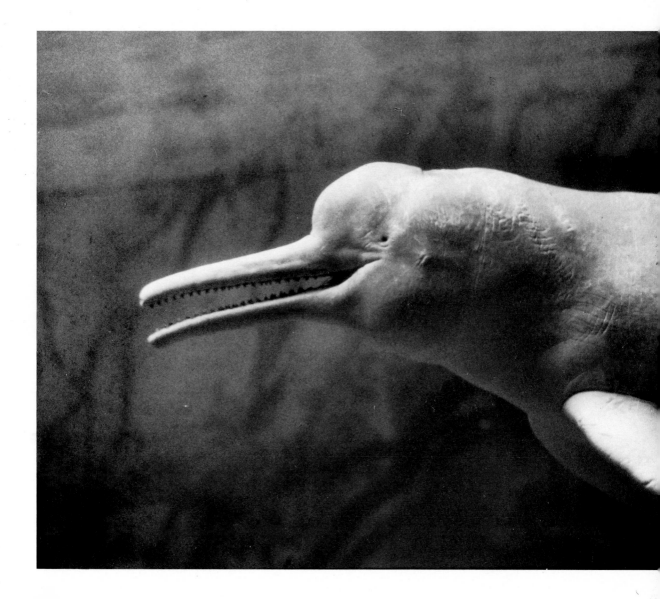

It usually feeds on fish near the deep river bottom. During high water it often swims into flooded forests and small lakes, where more varied food can be found. On top of its head is the blowhole. The dolphin rises to breathe about every 30 seconds.

With very few predators to worry about, the dolphins can swim, eat and play undisturbed. Another name for the mammal dolphin is "porpoise."

The *Takin*, which inhabits Asia,
looks like a composite of ox,
yak, gnu and goat antelope.
It lives above and below the
timberline on steep hillsides.
Despite its clumsy appearance,
which includes short legs with
dewclaws, it moves swiftly
on narrow paths and is a
skillful climber.

Takins are active and playful.
Some natives in Burma keep them as pets.

It is easy for the 600-pound takin to roll
a 200-pound tree stump.

The *Wolverine* is a most unusual mammal. No other animal can top its courage, cunning and strength. It can move obstacles too heavy for a man to lift and kill animals many times its size. The wolverine is also called the glutton because of its legendary appetite. Despite an average weight of only 35 pounds, its fury and temper are respected. Bears, big cats and packs of wolves hasten to abandon their meals when a wolverine challenges them.

After hunting for several hours,
the wolverine rests.
Reclining comfortably on a high,
rocky ledge, it grooms its long,
thick fur.

The wolverine is a good swimmer and occasionally fishes. It lives in a cave
and, to satisfy its great appetite, wanders tens of miles in search of food.

The *White Rhinoceros*, a native of Africa, is the largest land mammal after the elephants. It is not white, but rather different shades of brown or gray. It is much less aggressive than its relative the black rhino. White rhinoceroses live in pairs or small family groups and feed on grasses and other ground vegetation.

The *Bongo* is one of the most beautiful antelopes. It lives in the densest parts of the central African forests, areas rarely penetrated by humans.

During the day bongos rest. In the morning and afternoon they search for their favorite foods—tender leaves and roots.

To avoid entangling its horns in thick brush while running, the bongo lays them back, the tips touching its back. Some older animals have patches on their backs where the fur has been worn away.

Both male and female bongos have horns. Their frequently staged mock battles don't last long, and nobody gets hurt.

Two female *Addaxes* with their babies. Only one young is born yearly. The addax, the white antelope of Africa, lives in the driest parts of the Sahara Desert. It can go for most of its life without water, deriving moisture from the sparse vegetation of the desert. Addaxes live in small herds and travel long distances to feeding places. Because they are heavy and do not run swiftly, hunting by natives and drought have brought them close to extinction. In Israel, conservationists have established a refuge for animals that appear in the Bible. A small breeding group of addaxes already lives in the reserve.

The *Scimitar-horned Oryx* lives in the parts of the Sahara Desert where vegetation and water are available. However, as the grassy fringes give way to desert sand, the animal becomes rarer and rarer. Like the addax, it has also found refuge in Israel's extensive reserve.

Young *Musk Oxen* already know how to face danger. The defensive circle of the musk ox is an effective strategy against predators. Adult males form a front, protecting females and their young inside the circle. The habitat of the musk ox is the arctic tundra, in winter one of the coldest places on earth. The animals are well protected from freezing by a weatherproof double coat consisting of a long, heavy outer coat and an inner coat so thick that the severest cold or wind cannot penetrate it.

The *Cusimanse*, an African mongoose, travels in groups through the forest, never settling anywhere for long. This is an unusual way of life for a small animal, but moving may help the cusimanse avoid predators and also find a more varied diet. Reptiles, fruits, insects, small snails, eggs and berries are some of the animal's favorite foods. The cusimanse emits many different sounds to express pleasure, anger, and other emotions.

Reptiles
TORTOISES and TURTLES

Turtles spend most of their lives in water, while tortoises
are merely turtles that live on land.

The *Radiated Tortoise*
lives in a desolate,
sparsely populated part
of the southern end
of Madagascar.
Tribes living in this
rugged land sometimes
keep them as pets.
They consider them sacred
and do not allow them
to be killed or eaten.
They believe that
housing the tortoise
with their chickens
will keep disease away
from the chickens.
With little rainfall,
drought and a constant
food shortage, healthy
poultry is important
for the tribes' survival.

The *Galápagos Giant Tortoise* inhabits islands of the Pacific Ocean located 650 miles from mainland Ecuador. When explorers from Spain landed on the islands four centuries ago and saw the big tortoises (*Galápagos* in Spanish) they named the islands the Galápagos Archipelago. Many thousands of these harmless giants were killed as food by sailors of passing ships. It is not known how long the tortoises survive in the wild, but in captivity they live over 150 years. Close to extinction on their home islands, they are now protected by law.

Early in the morning the tortoise rests in the sun. Warmed up, it starts searching for food. In the afternoon it is time to sleep. Sleeping 16 hours a day, the tortoises lead a quiet, inactive, uneventful life.

The *Soft-shelled Turtle*, from China, bears a curious resemblance to a medieval knight in armor. An aquatic animal, it lives at the soft bottoms of rivers, lakes and other bodies of fresh water and is found throughout the world, except in Europe, Australia and South America. Its name describes it accurately, as it lacks a horny shield. Instead, its shell is covered with a soft, supple skin.

The three claws of the
webbed feet help the soft-shell
to hold onto a fish
or frog, to dig into soft
river sand and to scratch
an aggressor in defense.

The soft-shell appears to be
slow and defenseless
without a protective
shield. Far from it. If cornered
on land, it can run with
surprising agility to a
watery refuge. Because it
can disappear with
lightning speed in the
muddy bottoms of its
habitat, the soft-shell
is rarely seen.

Lying in shallow water,
it raises its neck
and breathes through
its long snout.
It also gets oxygen
from water and can
remain submerged
almost indefinitely.

The soft-shell is a ferocious fighter. Faced with danger, it darts its head
out, snapping. Behind its protruding lips are unusually strong jaws
capable of inflicting serious injury.

The soft-shell is able to outswim many predators.

LIZARDS

Horned lizards, skinks, geckos and monitors are all lizards.

The *Horned "Toad"* or Texas horned lizard is a lizard shaped like a toad. It inhabits the deserts of the U.S. and Mexico. Almost invisible against a background of sand and small rocks, in hot sunlight it dashes about in search of insects. When threatened, the little monster, bluffing, puffs up its usually flat body and raises itself to frighten the enemy.

When the sun begins to set
it is time to burrow
into the sand.

Soon only the head
is above ground

Two horns are still visible
where the "toad" has disappeared.

The sand cover is a welcome
protection from the cool
desert nights.

The *Shingleback Lizard* of Australia is a skink. Usually skinks are small; however, in Australia some species reach a length of 18–24 inches. The large shingleback is a slow mover. It feeds mostly on vegetation, such as blossoms and fruits, as well as snails. It rarely catches insects. It is diurnal, but very secretive. It hides easily between fallen trees or bushes. Little is known of its habits and behavior. Because its body has a "pinecone" on each end, the shingleback is called the two-headed lizard by natives. It is covered with large, overlapping shiny scales.

The broad tail looks remarkably like a head.

Bluffing, the shingleback raises its tail to the enemy. Should the false head be attacked, skink, minus tail, can escape. The tail will eventually grow back.

The *Komodo Dragon* is the largest living lizard in the world. Persistent rumors of giant "dragons" on Komodo Island in Indonesia were not taken seriously until 1912, when zoologists discovered and recognized this previously unknown species. Fossils of similar reptiles are found to be over 50 million years old. Some of these lizards measure 12 feet in length and weigh around 300 pounds. The Komodo dragon has no preferences in food: any animal, dead or alive, is a meal. Nobody knows the length of its life span in the wild. It does not live long in captivity.

Birds

The small, green *Hanging Parakeet* inhabits the Indo-Malayan region
and the Philippine Islands. It sleeps like a bat, suspended from a branch.
Even when awake it often maintains this position until it takes flight.

The *Brown Eared Pheasant* lives in the mountains of northeastern China. The name "eared pheasant" probably refers to the white earlike tufts on the sides of its head. Dwellers of the mountain region have hunted this rare bird close to extinction.

The *Kagu* is a fairly large bird found only in New Caledonia, an island in the South Pacific. When the French settled in New Caledonia, the flightless kagu became an easy catch for dogs, cats and other animals brought over by the settlers. The bird was hunted for food and sold in markets. Close to extinction, the kagu now inhabits mountains in a remote part of the island.

Male and female kagus look alike.
The crest is usually folded
back flat, giving the bird
a very unusual appearance.

When searching for food,
the kagu can run swiftly, with
crest and wings held close
to the body.

The kagu is mostly nocturnal, sleeping by day under rocks or bushes. Alert and active at night, it moves about with wings and tail dropped and its crest partly raised. Its evening and morning calls can be heard a mile away.

The kagu spreads its spectacular crest like a fan during courtship displays or when it is angry. Its feathers were once sold in Europe to hatmakers.

In courtship the male opens its wings in display, revealing his black and white markings.

The *White-necked Bald Crow* in Western Africa is rarely observed and has only recently been studied. It nests in deep forests on high hills, among boulders. Although it resembles a crow, it behaves more like a thrush, hopping high on its strong legs and scattering leaves and dirt as it searches for food. This bird is also known as the White-necked Rock Fowl.

The *Demoiselle Crane* of Africa
is a small, exquisite
bird. Its feathery "hairdo"
is unusual and charming.
The common crane and
the demoiselle are the only
cranes that visit Europe.
Demoiselles have been
observed in Denmark,
Spain, the British Isles
and Rumania.

The *Great Indian Hornbill* of Southeast Asia lives in the dense foliage of trees and mainly eats fruits and berries. The bird's long neck and bill are helpful in reaching hard-to-get fruit. The sharp bill is an effective weapon against enemies.

The hornbill is often tamed by natives who are amused by its clownish antics. Its large, long-lashed eyes and the horny casque on its bill are grotesque but fascinating. Most remarkable is the way the female hatches her eggs. She makes a nest in a hollow tree and seals herself in. She stays walled in for months, until her chicks are grown. No predator can rob the nest or kill the young hornbills. At least 20 times a day during this period the male feeds her and the chicks through a small slit. It has been estimated that the male brings about 24,000 meals to his family during the long confinement.

Rothschild's Starling lives in a small area of northern Bali. The beautiful, white, starling-sized birds have found protection in a Balinese wildlife reserve.

The *Japanese Crane* is Japan's "special national monument." For hundreds of years this crane was depicted on screens, prints and paintings by Chinese and Japanese artists. Several hundred of these graceful birds live on the island of Hokkaido.

The *Ocellated Turkey* of Central America is similar in size and behavior to the turkey of North America and Mexico. However, its bright blue neck and head, with coral-pink pimples and a yellow "crown," make it surprisingly different. This turkey can compete with the most colorful of birds.

The *King Vulture* of Central and South America is one of the largest flying birds in the world. It feeds on carrion (the flesh of dead animals), which it spots from the air. The king vulture is willing to fight for the meal it has spotted. Fights are not noisy because, lacking a syrinx—vocal organ—the bird is voiceless.

The average wingspread
of the king vulture is 6–8 feet.

INDEX